The Internet causes billions of images to appear on millions of computer monitors around the planet. From this galaxy of sight and sound will the face of Christ emerge and the voice of Christ be heard? For it is only when his face is seen and his voice heard that the world will know the glad tidings of our redemption. This is the purpose of evangelization.

—Pope John Paul II
Message of the Holy Father for the
36th World Communications Day
(May 12, 2002)

Technology Tools for Your Ministry

TIM WELCH

TWENTY
THIRD *23rd*
PUBLICATIONS

This book is dedicated to
Catherine Kallhoff, SSND.
It was Kate and her vision
that allowed me to explore new ways
of journeying with others.

Questions or comments? Email Tim Welch at cem.twelch@stcdio.org

Twenty-Third Publications
A Division of Bayard
One Montauk Avenue, Suite 200
New London, CT 06320
(860) 437-3012 or (800) 321-0411
www.23rdpublications.com

ISBN 978-1-58595-676-0
Library of Congress Catalog Card Number: 2007939470
Printed in the U.S.A.

CONTENTS

You know him. I know him. *Saturday Night Live* even had a recurring sketch about him: "Nick Burns, Your Company's Computer Guy." Your Nick may be a Barbara or a Pat, but the story is the same. You have difficulty opening an attachment to your email, and you call for help. Your version of Nick Burns walks in, reaches invasively over you to bang on a couple of keys on your keyboard. The attachment opens. He walks triumphantly away, saying sarcastically, "Was THAT so hard?" and once again you swear that technology is a necessary evil at best, and you are glad that your ministry is about people, not machines.

■　■　■

Several years ago, I was asked to facilitate a technology center for a national conference on catechesis. Apple, Inc. donated the use of twelve iBooks so that participants could check their email, and conference presenters would have a tool for demonstrating their online catechetical resources. It was amazing the number of participants who walked in, saw that the machines were not Windows based, and either sat down with a bit of a frown or simply walked away. And for many of the brave who sat down, they expressed further consternation at the presence of trackpads instead of mice. Meanwhile, upstairs, the conference's main theme was exploring the implications of a catechetical paradigm shift. We were at a conference to examine ways of moving others into a new catechetical model, and yet many participants couldn't shift to a different computer platform or input device!

■   ■   ■

A parish secretary called me about a web page on the diocesan site that wouldn't print correctly. I could tell she was becoming agitated as I tried to ascertain the exact problem. Finally, when I asked her to look for the version of Windows she was running, she said, "Can we end this phone conversation right now?" And we did. Could I have been gentler with her? Could I have said something right away to put her at ease, to convince her that I wasn't a Nick Burns trying to catch her at being computer illiterate? In spite of my best intentions, our conversation did nothing to move her forward into the use of technology and everything to make her feel less adequate as a parish minister.

These three examples remind us how important it is in the areas of technology to be kind to one another—neither defensive nor threatening. Those who are leaders in technology have to be careful not to intimidate others or judge those who won't try something new. "Experts" have to be gentle…oh so gentle, with their companions on this journey. Technology is a moving target. Each new day levels the playing field as it continually evolves with updates that not only move us into new territories, but often make it impossible for us to choose to stay in our comfortable zones. We are all novices to the newest update. Technology can teach us many lessons in humility and the need for community.

Humble Companions

Sr. Suzanne is a principal in a small, rural Catholic School. She has been an educational leader for many years, committed to teaching students with the help of computers, not teaching computers as a subject to

> Our primary
> vocation is to
> minister to one
> another in the
> gentlest, most
> life-giving way
> possible.

students. Every time the diocesan school technology leaders meet, she is there. And, even though she has been doing "educational technology" for about twenty years, she is there with an open mind and a willingness to learn from the youngest, even at seventy-nine. She uses the first Apple computer I've seen that runs both Windows and Mac OS X, and yet she doesn't hesitate to call for help when she is in "one mell of a hess!" Sr. Suzanne uses cutting-edge technology to print out and laminate card-sized digital pictures of all of her students for the bulletin board, and still calls the end of the USB cable a "doojy-bob." She is quick to praise the technical prowess of her colleagues in other schools and easily admits to being embarrassed if she misses an obvious fix in troubleshooting. What a model for ministry in general, and for the journey into a technologically-oriented world in particular.

This book is for the Sr. Suzannes in our church, to those who first and foremost consider themselves called to ministry. It is meant for the secretaries, the catechists, the pastoral leaders, council members, and other disciples of Jesus who want to proclaim the reign of God employing some of the tools modern technology has to offer. It is for the human and vulnerable people who want to be the best ministers possible, and who want to explore some of the powerful tools that technology has to offer. Our primary vocation is to minister to one another in the gentlest, most life-giving way possible. And let's promise one another not to allow the pursuit of technology to become an obsession or source of competition, but rather one of many means to an end, that of making present the reign of God.

1
TOGETHER IN A MEDIA WORLD

Who doesn't have a story about a youngster showing an adult how to do something tricky on a computer? Sr. Suzanne is twenty-five years my senior, and I show her many tricks on the computer, while my current mentor, David, is twenty-five years my junior. Some of us are "Digital Natives" and others are "Digital Immigrants," a phrase coined by Marc Prensky, in his book *On the Horizon*.

I really appreciate these labels because of the dynamics in my own family's use of technology and media. I have been involved in digital technology since 1983 or so, taking my first classes in BASIC and Pascal computer languages, while still working in a parish. My interest in technology, and using it as a tool in ministry, has grown ever since. Yet, I am a Digital Immigrant. I still print out my longer PDFs (covered later) and take them to my libraries (a.k.a. my desk, bedroom, or bathroom) to read more comfortably, and sometimes more privately.

And yes, I have fallen prey to Prensky's favorite example of the behavior of such an immigrant... I have called people to see if they got my email. Shame on me! But, did I mention that I type forty-five words a minute with few mistakes, far more than my father could?

> I have called people to see if they got my email. Shame on me!

By contrast, as my children grew up, it was apparent they had little interest in the computer. They didn't know what a serial port was, and they didn't care. But they are Digital Natives. Two of them own cell phones in lieu of landline telephones. They all use email as a natural part of their lives. And instant messaging (IM)? I have seen my youngest type 3,000 words per minute, mostly without vowels, to more people at the same time than I have friends—while doing her homework. In fact, all three of my daughters disliked keyboarding in school but became very proficient typists when they needed to IM their friends. And still I type forty-five words a minute.

This is the world we live in. Over thirty-five percent of the U.S. population was under the age of twenty-five in the 2000 census, and the vast majority of those are Digital Natives. Psychologist David Walsh of the National Institute on Media and the Family is demonstrating that these Digital Natives exhibit a difference in brain development because of the multi-media world in which

> We are called to go out to all ends of the world, which includes the world of the digital generation.

they live. As they view TV with its constantly changing stories from heavy drama to the joys of effective deodorant, as they listen to beat-laden music as they do homework, as they IM their friends while emailing teachers or classmates, their brains are growing in different ways. While it is true that Digital Immigrants grew up with the radio, television, and movies, the sheer number of opportunities afforded by digital advancements such as the multiplication of available channels and media venues has created a different environment for a different human being.

A few years ago I was at a presentation by Jesuit cultural historian John Staudenmaier of Detroit University. He spoke of a time when he was on retreat. One of his exercises consisted of reflecting on Jesus looking out at the world and saying "I love them, will you go out to them with me?" Now this was at the time of the military build up during the Vietnam era, and Staudenmaier could see a warplane factory outside his window. Surrounding the factory were rows of family houses at varying levels of construction. It was like a microcosm of modern society building its economy on a technology of war. In essence, he asked Jesus if he could love a world so bent on using this technology for purposes that seem foreign to the gospel. And he heard a voice saying something like "Yes. I love them. Now are you coming or not?"

Sometimes when I see teenagers answer their cell phones while ordering food at a restaurant, or instant messenging their friends instead of studying like I used to, or flipping from channel to channel in an effort to keep entertained, I can't help but wonder if Jesus can love this world too? Yet, I believe that Jesus is saying to us, today as always, that he loves the world, and is asking "are we coming or not?" He is inviting us to go with him into this world.

"Kids" do think differently than Digital Immigrants. They learn differently than Digital Immigrants. They speak a language differently than Digital Immigrants. And we are called to go out to all ends of the world, which includes the world of the digital generation.

2 COMPUTERS AND MINISTRY

When I first developed an interest in computers, I saw them as a tool for lightening my work by generating schedules and reports and budgets and bulletins, and that was about it. I didn't really see them as "media," as much as calculators and typewriters with memory. But now when I think of "media," I include computers and the many ways in which they are tools for consuming, critiquing, and creating media—and are thus essential to our ministry.

John Staudenmaier, in another address given some years ago, said that modern Christians, are:

1. In fact consumers of media

2. Required to be critiquers of media

3. Called to be creators of media

As obvious as these points seem, they really helped me to focus on the value of computers in education and in evangelization and catechesis.

I met an educator years ago who, after chatting about my Apple t-shirt, asked me why I supported Macintosh computers in our classrooms. I cited statistics on the number of hours children spend watching television. "American children, ages two to seventeen,

> Like teaching a child to write in order to become literate, we want to teach children to create media in order to become media literate.

watch television on average almost twenty-five hours a week or three and a half hours a day. Almost one in five watch more than thirty-five hours of TV each week" (D.A. Gentile and D.A. Walsh [2002, January 28]. "A normative study of family media habits." *Applied Developmental Psychology*, 23, 157-178). I told him that one of my goals as a consultant for educational technology is to encourage schools to teach media literacy skills. And, like teaching a child to write in order to become literate, we want to teach children to create media in order to become media literate. I shared with him the story of animations created in a vacation Bible school that, while obviously done by novices, taught the young students many things about what it takes to plan, draw out, and animate stories. It is through such activities that students could gain some insight into ways that media try to form (manipulate?) their minds. And I said that Macs were easier tools for that purpose, although not the only tool. My new friend admitted that he wanted to prompt a "Windows vs. Macintosh" debate, or even a discussion into the merits (or lack thereof) of teaching computers to youngsters, but he had never thought of computers in schools as being such powerful tools to teach media literacy. He understood that our students are already consumers of media, and that as they became creators themselves, they were opening themselves up to be more informed critics of the media they consume.

The *National Directory for Catechesis* (NDC) is filled with references to media, both in recognition of its impact on those we are asked to catechize as well as the need for catechists to teach our students to become media literate. Even before the NDC was published, catechetical leader and episcopal advisor to the National Conference for Catechetical Leadership (NCCL), Bishop Richard Malone, had this to say at a pre-publication symposium:

> Pay attention to media: its "formative" impact for better and for worse. Understand it, critique it, use it. In many ways, it can be argued that television and cinema are more formative influences than catechesis, especially in the lives of our children and young people. We must teach media literacy as well as learn to employ the media effectively in our faith formation efforts.

Undoubtedly, we consume media, perhaps too much many would say. But S. Rose Pacatte, FSP, and Rev. Richard Leonard, SJ, are two of many Catholic leaders who would espouse using our media, especially secular media, as a springboard for theological reflection. Leonard, in a February 3rd, 2006, podcast (www.spiritedtalktoday.com) points out that Jesus' stories are not religious in and of themselves: "If you want to know what the Kingdom's like, then there was a Father with two sons...," Leonard says of Jesus. "He knew the power of wonderful stories, and the media at its best is just a fantastic mode of telling stories." And Pacatte has written, with Peter Malone, the "Lights, Camera...Faith!" (Pauline Media) books that help readers reflect on the Lectionary cycles and Ten Commandments using modern motion pictures as the basis for discussion.

We also need to critique media. One needs only flip through the many, many channels of basic cable to get an idea of the varying levels of "storytelling" aimed at our

> It is also our task to actively create media to tell our story, to define our culture. This story is Jesus' story, the gospel story that proclaims the reign of God.

children as well as at us adults. It used to be said that if we didn't like programming, we should just switch the channel. In the days of four airwave-based channels, the audience had a strong voice in what was acceptable and what wasn't. A loss of a ten-percent market share could be devastating. But today, with so many stations to choose from, it takes a much smaller market share to keep an unhealthy program alive. And, although I may forbid that show from airing in my own house, the fact that other households allow it may contribute to the "culture of disrespect" that Dr. Walsh speaks of, and THAT does affect my family. We must be critics, and we must make our voices heard.

Dr. Walsh has also said, "Whoever tells the story defines the culture." It is also our task to actively create media to tell our story, to define our culture. This story is Jesus' story, the gospel story that proclaims the reign of God. I believe that we need to use the tools technology has to offer to tell our story and tell it well.

3

MATCHING TOOLS TO MINISTRIES

In the next several chapters, we will look at some of the basic tools that parish staffs (pastors, secretaries, pastoral associates, business administrators, etc.) might need. Then we will look at tools for catechists (directors of religious education, youth ministers, adult and young-adult faith formation ministers, etc.), and finally we will look at technology tools for disciples (all of us). Because it is impossible to present an exhaustive list, my hope is to provide a basic overview of some of the tools we need to use to integrate technology and ministry.

When I try to imagine how technology tools might help parish teams today, I think of mission statements. Parish teams have spent much effort and sometimes tears in crafting them. The mission statement of my own parish is similar to most that I've seen.

> We are a believing Community, called together
> by the Word of God, proclaiming Jesus as Lord.

His Word calls us to be welcoming, serving, compassionate, and open to diversity.

Our purpose as a Christian People is to facilitate, through worship, service to others, fellowship, and education, the Kingdom of God.

— Church of Saint Paul,
Saint Cloud, Minnesota

How can technology tools help parishes like mine to achieve their mission? One key way is by helping them to better communicate it. Sr. Angela Ann Zukowski, MHSH, of the University of Dayton, made four points about communication in an address to the National Association of Catechetical Media Professionals (NACMP) in 2002:

1. Ministers need to be experts in communication.

2. Communication is not a luxury, but the essence of ministry formation.

3. We are not only the messenger, but also the message.

4. The health of our parish is reflected in the quality and depth of the flow of communication.

The biggest problem I see today within diocesan and parish staffs is the breakdown of communication. Conversely, where I see a safe environment in which to foster solid, open communication, I see a strong diocesan parish or school team. The following are tools that I would choose to foster healthy communication.

I want...
The Right Computer

Obviously you will need a computer for much of what follows. I receive many calls asking for advice on what computers and peripherals (printers, projectors, etc.) to purchase. What follows are my recommendations from well over twenty years of making many good decisions (Okay, some bad decisions too!).

Platform (Operating Systems) Considerations. Although I will limit my discussion to Microsoft Windows and Mac OS X, I am reading that more and more schools are turning to Linux as their OS. Linux and its applications are quite cost effective (read "free" in most cases) if there is technical expertise to employ it.

If John Lennon wrote his song "Imagine" today, I believe he would have added:

> *Imagine just one platform!*
> *I wonder if you could...*
> *No Microsoft or Apple;*
> *It's for the common good!*

If you want to see passion, google "Mac vs. PC." Be sure to include the quotation marks. I came up with 1,170,000 results. I have rarely seen so much passion.

In all fairness, both Microsoft (Windows) and Apple (Macintosh) have survived for many years because they produce good operating systems (OS). When choosing an OS, consider the following in making a decision:

1. **Check with your diocesan office.** They may require certain reports that demand specific programs and therefore a specific operating system.

2. **Parishes can successfully use either platform and can easily use both.** More and more software produce documents compatible with either platform. I am writing this sentence in Microsoft Word for Macintosh, and it can be read by all modern versions of Microsoft Word for Windows (and Corel's WordPerfect and other programs for that matter).

3. **Choose the software first, then the platform and machine.** For example, ParishSOFT LLC, Logos, and Parish Data Systems provide some fine software that work only on a Windows computer. If you need business or financial software, the Windows world has more choices. If you need to do a lot of graphics, design, and multimedia work, the Macintosh world still has the edge. It may be that the secretary needs Windows while the youth minister prefers a Macintosh.

4. **Technical support is a prime consideration.** If something should go wrong or you need help in accomplishing your task, you need someone you can turn to at a moment's notice. Is your local expert good with Windows or Macintosh or both?

5. **Macintosh computers can run Windows operating**

systems now with the Intel chip and the appropriate enabling software, but you need to buy a full copy of Windows, whereas it comes free with a PC.

> Computers are just tools to do what is important, which in this case is ministry!

6. **Comfort Level.** Choose a machine that provides you with the greatest comfort level. Computers are just tools to do what is important, which in this case is ministry!

7. **Price.** While it is true that it is possible to buy a Windows machine for less money than a Macintosh, when you match feature for feature, the cost difference disappears. If all you are doing is word-processing, spreadsheets, and email, you can easily get by with an inexpensive PC running Windows. If you want quality sound, improved graphics, recording capabilities, a built-in camera, CD/DVD burning with included software, costs are competitive.

Once a young boy asked a karate expert who would win if he sparred with a heavyweight boxing champion. The wise Sensei replied, "A master of any art is hard to defeat." The same is true with computer platforms. If you use a platform you have "mastered," or have a computer "sensei" who can teach you a certain platform, use that one. But make sure the software you use allows for cross-platform communication. Most mainstream software is available for both Windows and Macintosh. It is all about communication.

Other Considerations

1. **Desktop or Laptop.** If you need mobility, get a laptop. Ask about the battery's life expectancy, replacement cost, and environmental impact. If you don't need mobility, a desktop or tower computer is less expensive, faster, and more reliable. Plus, the monitor, keyboard, and mouse are often easier to work with, although many people attach such external devices to their laptop for comfort.

2. **Hard-Drive Space.** This is the device that stores all your information when the machine is turned off. Bigger is better, but if you are SURE you will be doing only business work like number crunching and word processing, you can save money by going smaller. You can always add a larger drive.

3. **Memory.** (Random access memory, or RAM). These are the chips that help the computer think, but only when the machine is turned on. Get more than the minimum memory required by your software or you will be frustrated. I've never heard anyone say, "Dang, I have too much RAM!"

4. **Speed.** (Measured in hertz, or clock ticks per second.) Roughly speaking, a computer can issue one command per every two clock ticks. At two gigahertz, my laptop performs about a billion commands per second. If you are doing heavy-duty graphics or video editing (great tools for catechesis and youth or young-adult ministry) faster is better. If you are doing mostly business-oriented work, slower is where you can save money.

Other Considerations

1. **Backup Systems.** This can be as simple as a "flash drive." ($20 for one gigabyte is not unusual.) Use these for quick backups. They are too volatile to be used as a permanent solution. Or use an external hard drive that can be plugged into your USB or Firewire port. It is best to have software that regularly backs up your work for you, but in any case, remember, if you don't want to lose it forever, back it up.

FLASH DRIVE

EXTERNAL HARD DRIVE

2. Malware (Virus, Spyware, etc.) Protection.
Macintosh computers are less prone to attacks from malicious viruses, but there are viruses that affect both platforms. It is wise to invest in protection, especially if you are running Windows.

3. Printers. You have several choices:

- My top recommendation for most parishes is a networkable color laser printer. Prices have dropped, and you don't have to do color all the time.

- Ink jet printers are a good choice for parishes on very tight budgets. However, you will wind up spending a lot on ink cartridges. A good place to buy inexpensive cartridges is www.lasermonks.com.

- If your parish also needs a copier, consider purchasing one that can also serve as a networked printer. A copier/printer allows you to print thousands of pages at a time and to use all the normal copier features such as two-sided printing and stapling.

4. Scanner. If you need to scan many documents or images (like photos or slides), you can purchase a fast, quality scanner for under $500. For an occasional scan, you can buy one for under $100. You can also buy ink-jet printer/copier/scanner combinations for under $100. You can even add fax capability for a little more.

I want...
To Produce Documents
(letters, bulletins, homilies)

Everyone understands paper. No matter what word processor you use (including a Bic pen), once you get it on paper, you can hand the paper to someone else, and your message is readable. Still, paper wasn't always the only choice:

> Students today depend upon paper too much. They don't know how to write on slate without getting chalk dust all over themselves. They can't clean a slate properly. What will they do when they run out of paper?
>
> —Principals' Association, 1815

If we want to communicate, we don't want to receive an "I couldn't open the file" call from anyone. Thus the need for Microsoft Office compatibility. If everyone had an Office version for Windows or for the Macintosh, there would be great harmony in sharing Microsoft Word files, Microsoft Excel files (spreadsheets for finance), and Microsoft PowerPoint (presentations). With the exception of a few font differences, you can open the same file on either platform, edit it, and send it to a friend who runs the other platform.

Word-Processing Considerations

1. **Buying Microsoft Office is the simplest solution.** You can buy Microsoft Word by itself, but most people also want Excel and PowerPoint, which are included in Mircosoft Office.

2. **You don't need Microsoft Office for compatibility.** But then, make sure you know how to "be compatible" with it using the software you own (see sidebar). Some people prefer a different company, a different price, or a different learning curve than that offered by Office. Corel's Wordperfect Office X3 (WordPerfect X3, Quattro Pro X3 and Presentations X3) and Apple's iWork (Pages, Numbers, and Keynote) are but a couple of the many applications you can buy that allow you to import or export your work as Microsoft Word (and other Office) files. And there are free alternatives, such as Open Office, Zoho, and NeoOffice, although you may need a little tech-savvy help to get them up and going. Go to Google (also known as "googling") and type in "Office Alternatives" for lots of opinions and information.

3. **Buy from software vendors that sell to non-profits.** Googling "software for non-profits" can lead you to companies that specialize in this. I checked with a colleague to get a recommendation of companies like Consistent Computer Bargains, Inc. (www.1ComputerBargains.com) and saved a lot of money.

Importing and Exporting Word Documents

If you cannot open a received file by double-clicking on it, try one of the following:

1. Drag and drop it on your word processing application.

2. Right click (control-click in Macintosh) and choose the "Open with…" command in the contextual window and choose your word processing program.

3. Open your word-processing program, and choose the appropriate "file format" from the pull down menu in the File>Open menu command. Choosing "All available" often works well. The example below is similar to most Windows or Macintosh programs. Exporting is similar, look for the File Type or Format menu in the File>Save As… dialogue box.

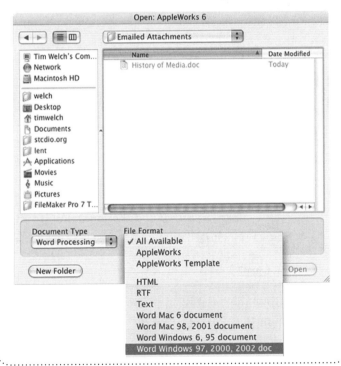

4. Use common fonts. I love the Papyrus font. However, if I send a file that uses it to someone who doesn't have it, the computer will find a substitute font that may throw off alignment or display strange characters. Stick with Arial or Helvetica for sans serif fonts (fonts where capital "i"s look like straight vertical lines) or Times or Times New Roman for serif fonts (where capital "i"s look like I-beams). Your file won't be as much fun to create, but it will be more compatible—this is all about communication.

> The Papyrus font has a certain classical feel for specific occasions.

I want...
To Use the Web

1. Get connected.

   • Call the local telephone company, cable company, and other more specialized internet service providers (ISPs) and get prices. Make sure they know you are a church and therefore non-profit. Some local church members can be very generous in their rates if they are ISPs.

   • Get the fastest connection you can afford. Although you can still get by with a modem connected to your telephone line, it is really too slow for most of today's needs. I updated my Microsoft Word program this morning connected to the Internet via cable. The software was downloaded in less than two minutes. The *download* web page said it would take three hours and 21 minutes if I had dial-up speed of 56 kbps. Speed is particularly important if you want to connect more than one computer to the internet.

> Get the fastest connection you can afford.

2. Once connected, launch the free web browser that came with your computer. Internet Explorer for Windows and Safari for the Macintosh will both provide a satisfactory surfing (browsing the web) experience, but do check out other browsers like the cross-platform Firefox. They each handle text and graphics somewhat differently, and soon you will find a preferred surfing application.

3. Point your browser to Google (jargon for "go to www.google.com"), put in some keywords for your favorite subject like "parish ministry," and let the surfing begin!

Common Configuration for a Small-office Network

Matching Tools to Ministries

Internet

Cable Modem
or
DSL connection

Router
(So more computers
can be online)

Switch

4

EMAIL, DATA, AND OTHER ESSENTIALS

Email is still a relatively new phenomenon, especially in terms of using it wisely and effectively. I know of one pastor who refused to allow email in any of his three parishes. On the other hand, there is a guy who still has five hundred and seventy email messages that he has scanned, ascertained that they were not critical, and saved them to be "dealt with later" (that be me). There is something wrong with that picture too!

Getting an email account

1. **Call your Diocesan Office.** Some dioceses have an email "environment" that offers email accounts along with other communication tools. FirstClass is one of many such software solutions. Go to www.firstclass.com/FC81 for more information. These are great for offering an "Internet area" that is secure and allows for multiple levels of communication between parishes and schools. I can

> Email is becoming more and more integrated with other programs.

imagine a pastoral associate reading "Coworkers in the Vineyard of the Lord" (USCC Publishing) and sending out an email to her group address of all other pastoral associates in the diocese asking them to read it and write a short reaction to it in the pastoral associates online conference room so it can be read by others anytime. Or I think of a parish secretary who found a funny, poignant, royalty-free cartoon online. She could drop it in a public "secretary's resource folder" to be downloaded by other secretaries for their bulletins. It is not surprising that these very powerful tools are very expensive—to buy and to support. But it is all about communication.

2. **POP Accounts.** It IS all about communication, but this is our Church, and we tend to shy away from solutions that cost a lot of money. Enter POP (Post Office Protocol) accounts. Usually, when you sign up with a service provider, you receive one to five email accounts. Then the internet service provider gives you the information needed to set up your account in the email program that probably came for free with your computer (Mail on the Macintosh, and now Windows Mail, an updated version of

Outlook Express, for Windows). Often you will also get a web address that you can go to when you are traveling, and you can check your email using any web browser. When you check your email with your email program (called an email *client*), that email is downloaded to your computer and removed from the email server at the internet service provider. Then you can file messages away, and search for old emails very quickly at any time.

Email is becoming more and more integrated with other programs. For example, if you click on a mail address on a web page, you get an addressed "new mail" window ready to fill out and send off. Or, if you have FileMaker Pro (see below), you can create a database with email addresses, do a query on a subset of your constituents, and send an email to them. At my office, I will do a "find" on all DREs, write a note in a single "global" field, and push a button. FileMaker Pro then goes to the first record, populates an email message with my note, and sends it through my email client. Then it goes to the second DRE found, and sends that, and so on. The effect is that I can have a dynamic set of group addresses, and, since one email goes out at a time, the recipients' internet service providers don't sense my email as a piece of spam (junk mail). Plus, I can send email messages that have certain "mail merge" qualities, such as including the recipient's first name.

3. **Free email accounts.** There are many free email services. All three of my daughters have either "Gmail" (from Google) or "Hotmail" (from Microsoft) accounts. They are free, can be accessed from anywhere through a web browser, and have served my daughters well. They also show lots of advertising, and do not interact as well with applications like FileMaker Pro.

4. **Domain Names.** Check with your Internet Service Provider about obtaining a domain name for your parish or school. It is the address used by the Internet to locate your email mailbox and/or a web page. Stclouddiocese.org is the domain name for an email address of *yourname*@stclouddiocese.org or web address of www.stclouddiocese.org. A normal price for a domain name is about $15 per year.

Considerations in using email

1. How to use email

- The hardest thing is setting up the account, and that has gotten much easier. Your internet service provider will give you full directions, but basically you just tell your email client application:

  » What to call your account. "Dad's Account" would work for me at home.

  » Your email address.

» Your full name. This will appear on messages you send out.

» Incoming mail server. Your client has to know where to get your messages. A typical setting is mail.*yourISP*.com (or net)

» Your username. This is your email address to the left of the "@" sign.

» Your password.

» Your outgoing mail server. Usually this is the same as the incoming server, but sometimes it is smtp.*yourISP*.com (or net). Outgoing mail is a different thing than incoming, and it uses a different protocol called simple mail transfer protocol (SMTP).

• Usually your email automatically checks for new mail when you launch the program, and you can set it to check regularly. Any more often than five minutes can be overkill, and there is no need to tie up the network.

Delete Reply Reply All Forward New Mailboxes Get Mail Junk

MACINTOSH MAIL ICONS

• The commands in email are straightforward and often seen as icons on your tool bar or at the top of your window. Following along the tool bar from Mail above, you click on a message and then, respectively: delete it, reply to only the sender, reply to the sender and all others he or she had listed in the "to:" field or "cc:" field (for carbon copy), forward the message to someone else (including attachments), compose a new message, reveal mailboxes and archived folders, check mail manually, and mark an email as "Junk" to teach the software to mark similar messages as spam.

WINDOWS MAIL ICONS

2. Email etiquette.

- Email is a unique form of communication. Be brief, but polite. Use titles, "please" and "thank you." If you are writing more than three paragraphs, it may be better to call the person.

- Typing in all caps is considered shouting. AVOID IT!

- Remember that people cannot hear nuanced tones in email. My dry sense of humor doesn't always work online. I have to be careful.

- Don't send out anything that you can't have the world know, even if you think you are only sending it to your most trusted friend. One time, after a romantic interlude, an educator mistakenly sent a note meant only for her boyfriend to many people. She was unemployed after that and very embarrassed.

- You address an email by entering one or more comma-separated addresses in the "to:" field. You can do the same in the cc: field to indicate "carbon copies." In both cases, all recipients see who the email is sent to. However, if you don't want to "give away" who will receive it, address it to yourself, and list all the recipients in the "bcc:" field. You get a copy for your records, and they don't see who else got the message since it is a "blind carbon copy." There is also the advantage that Malware (viruses) won't be able to harvest those addressees.

> Don't send out anything that you can't have the world know.

- Attachments
  - » If an attachment is large (over one megabyte in file size), it may not be delivered. Beware: a photo can easily be 1.5 or more megabytes.
  - » If you receive an attachment, don't open it unless you know the sender. You may be launching a virus or other destructive software.

Making a Large File Smaller for Email Attachments

To make a file easier to email, or fit onto a smaller disk, Windows and Macintosh users can compress one or more files into a "zip" file.

1. Click on the file(s) or folder you want to compress.

   a. Right click on the selection and choose "Send To>Compressed (zipped) folder" (Control-Click on a Mac>Create "Archive of ..." on a Mac)

   b. You will see a new file with a ".zip" at the end of the filename.

2. Your original file(s) or folder remains intact.

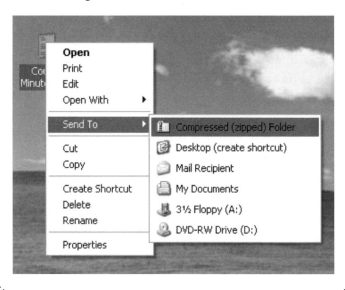

To "Unzip" a file:

1. Double-click on the zipped file.

    a. On a Mac, the de-compressed file or folder will appear in the same folder as the zipped file.

    b. In Windows, a window will open up showing the contents of the zipped file. Click on "Extract all files," or drag the file or files you want to a location of your choosing.

2. Your compressed file remains intact and can be "unzipped" again.

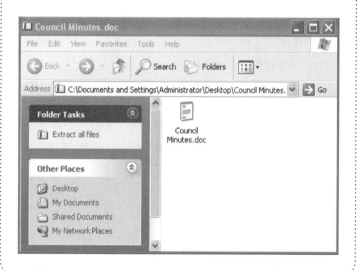

Likewise, it may be good to let someone know you are sending an attachment (a "warning" email perhaps, or even a phone call makes sense in some cases), so that you don't cause him or her any concern.

» Make sure the recipient is able to open the attachment. If you don't know what software he or she is using, create a PDF (Portable Document Format) file (see page 44) and send it with a link to Adobe's free Acrobat Reader.

- Never respond to spam (unsolicited junk mail). I know *you* won't, but somebody does. And if only a tiny fraction of one percent reply, it keeps spammers in business.

- Do not post your email address on a web page. The "mailto" link ("click here to send email to...") has an email address in the code of the page, even if it isn't visible. Programs called robots go through the web and collect these addresses for spammers.

I want...
A Tool for Managing Numbers

Microsoft Excel, or comparable applications like Corel's Quattro Pro or Apple's Numbers, is a great tool for keeping books and lists to serve a variety of purposes. It is called a "spreadsheet" because it contains a grid of discrete fields (cells) of information that are "spread" out like a newspaper or ledger. While it is possible to keep a list of people, their vital information, and other data like pledges or volunteer committees, the real purpose of a spreadsheet is to store and analyze numbers. This tool is ideal for creating a budget and charting the figures.

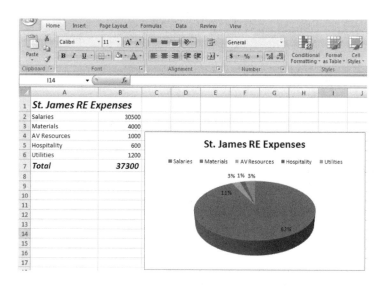

A spreadsheet is also a perfect tool for constructing "what if" scenarios. For example, instead of putting salaries into a parish budget, you put in formulas that reflect salaries elsewhere on the spreadsheet multiplied by a cost of living figure. Then, by changing only the cost of living "index," you can see the differences in the bottom line of the parish budget.

I want...
A Tool for Managing Data

Creating your own database

While some people use Excel for all of their simple data handling, most find a need for a more robust solution when it comes to data about people. Enter the database.

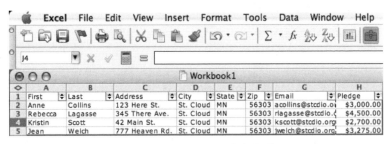

LIST IN AN EXCEL DOCUMENT

Going beyond Excel's limits

Most people would agree that Excel is the tool of choice when it comes to crunching numbers and building charts. But when your needs become more sophisticated and you want to add graphics, print professional reports, perform complex searches and sorts, or share your data across a workgroup, it's time to consider a database solution. Used together,

FileMaker and Excel give you everything you need to get the most out of your data.

—www.filemaker.com/products/technologies/excel.html

FileMaker Pro is a database program that has won many awards by combining power and ease of use. I prefer it because it works on both Windows and Macintosh. While a database is not as easy to create as a spreadsheet, once finished you have a powerful tool for ministry. I think of a database as an interactive Rolodex that can generate reports, lists, merged form letters, envelopes, and labels. With FileMaker Pro, I can generate emails and PDF files using the data in my file. The possibilities are almost

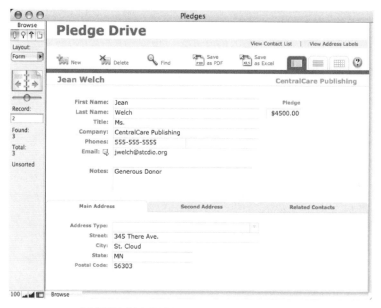

RECORD IN A FILEMAKER PRO DOCUMENT

> Think of a database as an interactive Rolodex that can generate reports, lists, merged form letters, envelopes, and labels.

endless. My "do list," expense report, check request form, purchase orders, and address book are FileMaker Pro solutions. My media center's video collection, with multi-paragraph fields for item description and catalogue publishing, is kept on FileMaker Pro. A liturgist can have a catalogue of songs, with sound files embedded so that he or she can listen to them to ascertain the correct version. An administrator can store files in container fields to catalogue pastoral council minutes or spreadsheets of bygone budgets. A youth minister can have a file of high schoolers that contains not only their home addresses and photos, but also a button that will show their Facebook profile on the web. And network sharing is built right in. If a secretary has a membership file open on her computer, the pastor can connect to it if he has a copy of FileMaker Pro. Any changes he makes are made directly in the secretary's file.

There are other databases to consider, such as Microsoft Access and Corel Paradox, but these are only for the Windows environment, and are not as easy to use as FileMaker Pro.

As previously mentioned, database authoring has a steeper learning curve than spreadsheet use. My dream would be for parishes to work together to agree on a database application and collaborate in creating databases such as those described above that would suit their needs. Many parishes reinvent the wheel when it comes to data handling.

Buying Pre-made Database Solutions

When you buy a database application, you still have to create your "solution," or database file, to do what you want. Although they usually come with some "templates," or generic ready-to-use files like "Contact Management," most parishes would need to adapt them extensively to fit their ministerial needs. There are "turnkey" applications that are written specifically for parish use that would eliminate the need for authoring. These programs can be expensive and may require an annual fee for support and updates. But some of these programs have integrated many functions like contributions, pledges, and membership into one easy-to-use package. Plus there may be some very powerful online features such as web space, scheduling, and announcements. Googling "parish software" will bring up links to sites for companies such as ParishSoft and Parish Data Systems, both of whom have been around for some time.

I want...
To Share Digital Documents

Paper is still the main medium for hand-written letters, bulletins to be handed out after liturgy, and books for the beach. But what if we wanted to email an agenda of a parish council meeting, or a full-color invitation to the pastor's twenty-fifth anniversary celebration? What if we wanted to save postage and trees? If everyone had all the same programs and all the same fonts and the same computer platform, sharing files would be easy. I could create a beautiful newsletter in an expensive desktop publishing program like QuarkXpress, and you could open it and read it in your copy of "Quark." At $700 or more per license, however, most parishes can ill afford this luxury. Years ago Adobe developed a technology to create documents that would look the same on any computer. This is called the Portable Document Format (PDF). PDFs can be read using the free Adobe Reader (www.adobe.com/products/acrobat/readstep2.html), and other compatible programs like Apple's Preview. A PDF can maintain the font, layout, and graphics of a document so that it looks as the author originally intended it to look. It cannot be altered, however.

Creating a PDF

1. Windows

- Google "Creating PDFs in Windows." The results will display a number of free utilities

Finding information in PDFs

Our diocesan directory is generated by FileMaker Pro and is on the web. Thus it is always available, saves publication costs, and makes regular updating easier. People can still print it out, but I suggest they launch it from their desktop every morning so they can quickly search it by pressing CTRL-F (Windows) or Command-F (Macintosh) and entering criteria.

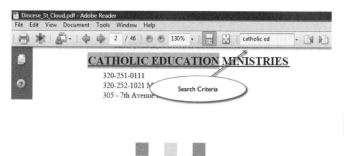

Copying text from PDFs

Although you cannot edit information in Adobe Reader (You need Adobe Acrobat Professional for that), you can select and then copy text from a document by pressing CTRL-C (Windows) or Command-C (Macintosh), and pasting it into your word processing program for editing.

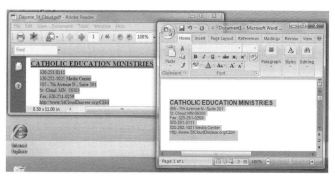

that will allow you the option of choosing a PDF document creator in the print dialogue box instead of a printer. You can then save the PDF on your computer. Many of these programs are free, and I hear good things about PDF995. With this program, you may see some advertising launched automatically on your web browser, but it is a small price to pay for a freebie. Paying their reasonable request of $9.95 will disable this "feature." Also, you can save a document as a PDF in Office 2007 with a free "add-in" from Microsoft.

2. Macintosh

- Go to File>Print as usual and select the built-in "Save as PDF" option under the PDF button, and save your document on your computer.

I want...
To Do My Office Work Once, *and Only Once*

As mentioned before, if you don't want to lose your work, back up your hard drive. Very often I hear people bemoan, "It worked yesterday!" Hard drives are electro-mechanical devices, and just as a burned out light bulb "worked yesterday," so too can electronics fail in an instant. Hard drives store information written in billions of magnetic bits on a metal platter the diameter of a small donut. It isn't amazing that problems can arise—it is amazing that it works at all. If you think you may forget to manually backup by copying important files to another drive, buy a backup program that will do it for you.

> Just as a burned out light bulb "worked yesterday," so too can electronics fail in an instant.

Backup Considerations

1. There is a difference between simply copying your files and truly "backing them up" with a program. If you simply copied the same document over and over to an external disk as a safety precaution, you would have copied the changes to the document as well. If someone should need a copy of a document, as it was a month before recent changes were made, you would be out of luck. You can set many backup programs to add changed documents to the backup catalog instead of replacing them.

2. Check out backup software reviews on the web sites of major PC or Macintosh magazines like *PCWorld* (www.pcworld.com) and *MacWorld* (www. macworld.com).

3. Have at least two drives and alternate their use. If something should happen during data transfer, you still have a recent copy of your files.

4. If your data is mission critical, store your backup disks off-site. This can be as simple as agreeing with a neighboring parish to house each other's backup drive.

5. There are online backup services where your files are saved to a secure drive through the Internet for a fee. This eliminates the need for off-site storage or extra drives.

I want...
Good, Inexpensive Training

You CAN Read the Manual

As a lay minister and technical instructor, I find myself in continual need of training. In 1991, I did the unthinkable. I read a computer program manual from beginning to end. It had approximately two hundred pages for Microsoft Works 2.0. Then I upgraded to Works 3.0 and only skimmed its manual, looking for new features. Then version 4.0 was released, and I simply played with it on my computer. I didn't feel the need to read the manual. I learned a few things about software training:

1. **You CAN read a manual...** if you can find it, that is. Now they often come as PDFs on installation disks. Make sure you check to see how long they are before printing them! Trainers get paid big bucks because

they do read the manual, and most manuals are in English and do make sense.

2. **Read the shortest manual you can find for your favorite program.** In learning one program well, you begin to become accustomed to how other programs work. For example, if you learn to import a text file into Microsoft Word, you will feel more comfortable importing an Excel file into FileMaker Pro.

3. **Keep the manual on your nightstand.** Although it works as a sleep aid, you will also find little tidbits that will get you excited. I have a 777-page book about FileMaker Pro which I will read until I learn one new thing. This new piece of information almost always makes my data-keeping life easier.

4. **Buy a third party book about your software** if you cannot print out the manual or cannot stand the manual. They are understandably expensive, given the fact that they will be out of date in about eighteen months. But they are less expensive than a live trainer and can be referred to in the future. The "For Dummies" series (www.dummies.com), the "Missing Manual" series (www.missingmanuals.com), and the "Visual Quickstart" series (www.peachpit.com) are some of my favorites.

5. **Commit yourself to training.** It is worth the effort.

Okay, What If You CAN'T Read the Manual?

1. **Form a "User's Group."** Meet regularly with other staff members and teach one another. There is always a guru willing to share tricks and tips. The Catholic school technology personnel in our diocese are teachers, librarians, and even retired parishioners who either volunteered or "were volunteered" to take on the digital world. They meet two or three times per year to share problems and successes and to learn new applications.

2. **Check out online resources.** Google "Microsoft Word Tutorials." There are many schools that post instructions for using applications that their teachers are required to use. Plus, there are many online training services like Atomic Learning (www. atomiclearning.com), an internationally known training site because of its wide selection of video-based tutorials.

3. **Check with your diocese and neighboring dioceses.** Our diocese offers training for $25 per three-hour class. We can do this because of the generosity of the teachers and of the schools that open up their labs at a nominal cost. With some business-oriented training costing $400 per day or more, parish staff can travel some distance and still save money.

4. **Take classes offered at a hotel near you.** You may have received flyers for two days of professional

training held at hotel conference centers. My understanding is that these are worth the money corporations pay for them. They are an opportunity for staff to get away and concentrate in an intense learning environment. But parishes often don't have that kind of money. If you are interested in such an opportunity, make sure that there are computers available for hands-on training, unless your learning style is such that you can absorb demonstrations by passively watching.

5. **Check with your local college,** community education, high school, or vocation-technical school. They typically offer great courses at a reasonable cost.

6. **Commit yourself to training.** It is worth the time.

The purpose of these tools is to minister more effectively. If the reign of God is about relationships with God and neighbor, each tool should enhance relationship building. If we can communicate better both locally and globally and make more time for communication, we have succeeded. I wish I could remember the citation of a study that said computer-savvy teachers saved an average of thirty-nine minutes of office time per day. If we can save that much time, we would have about four weeks more per year to be Church. It is worth the upfront time to learn these tools.

5 TOOLS FOR DRES AND CATECHISTS

According to the *National Directory for Catechesis*, there are six tasks of catechesis:

1. Catechesis promotes knowledge of faith.

2. Catechesis promotes a knowledge of the meaning of the Liturgy and the sacraments.

3. Catechesis promotes moral formation in Jesus Christ.

4. Catechesis teaches the Christian how to pray with Christ.

5. Catechesis prepares the Christian to live in community and to participate actively in the life and mission of the Church.

6. Catechesis promotes a missionary spirit that prepares the faithful to be present as Christians in society.

These tasks form the basis for the technological tools I would choose as a catechist. And since education is a major part of that ministry, I find it helpful to turn to pioneers in the K-12 world of education to see how they have effectively integrated technology into learning.

Jerome Berg of Livermore, California, spent thirty-four years teaching high-school English. In a presentation he gave at an Apple Executive Briefing in June of 2007, he shared one way he used Keynote, Apple's version of PowerPoint. In preparation for a unit on John Steinbeck's *Of Mice and Men*, Berg surfed the web for still clips from movies of the book, which he put into a presentation. He then showed it to his class with no other introduction. He asked his students to describe what they saw. Of course, they saw a big man who didn't seem too bright. And they saw a smaller man who seemed to care about his larger companion. Then there was the beautiful woman. Berg asked his students to construct a possible storyline. Then he passed out the books and invited them to see if they were correct. Rather than giving them a chance to roll their eyes at the prospect of reading yet another book, he immediately

Don't simply use the presentation software as an expensive overhead.

engaged them in the story and invited them to verify their intuitions.

What a master teacher! He didn't simply use his presentation software as an expensive overhead.

I want...
A Presentation Aid

Almost every catechist has heard of PowerPoint or Keynote. It is like an overhead with slides that can contain text, pictures, sounds, and movies. You can animate the items so they fly in from any direction, twist, turn, and make sounds as they move. You can show a slide on a large screen and at the same time see your notes on your computer monitor. For a youth council planning session, for example, you can type out action steps while the presentation is running. In class, it would be great to show artistic interpretations of Jesus throughout history while discussing Church history and Christological developments. Or more simply, you can display photos of the Church as you talk about the ambo. You can talk about discipleship and show a clip from *Remember the Titans*. You can project the lyrics of a song written by your fourth graders. And, remembering that the human brain remembers best by teaching others, you can have your students (including adolescents and adults, of course) create a presentation for another group. After the presentation is complete, you can save it as a movie or a web site for future generations.

Tips for a PowerPoint or Keynote Presentation

1. **Don't be afraid to use the templates provided.** It is fun to create slides yourself, but it is more important to have readable presentations if your graphic eye is not yet developed.

2. **Select colors that work well together.** Test your presentation on a suitable wall or screen. The colors you see on your computer may look different when projected.

3. **Use animations elegantly:** Although text can move in many different ways, ask yourself if the motion is an enhancement or distraction.

4. **Make sure your computer can handle multimedia embedded in your slides.** There are few features as powerful as a well-chosen audio or visual clip, or as frustrating as a song or movie that halts sporadically during playback.

5. **Use graphics wisely.** Rather than listing statistics on world hunger, it may be more powerful to have a photo of a big-eyed child with a simple bowl of rice and beans.

6. **Maintain appropriate font size:** Some would say that a 14-point font is the minimum. A rule of thumb is to print a slide, and place it on the floor. If you can read it easily as you stand above it, the print is large enough.

7. **Use fonts consistently:** Different fonts, although *FUN*, can be annoying.

8. **Don't use too much text:** Six short sentences should be the maximum, unless of course you are projecting a document, like a pastoral council constitution, for discussion.

9. **Don't simply read the text you have.** This offends some audiences. A handout would be better.

10. **Remember:**

White Space Is Our Friend

What You Need to Do "a PowerPoint"

Tools for DREs and Catechists

1. **A mobile computer.** While a desktop computer is best for office work, a laptop works best for moving your presentation to your class area or for allowing other catechists to use it in their learning and prayer environments. Since many presentations contain video clips or music, spend the extra money to get a powerful-enough laptop to handle multimedia well.

2. **A projector.** Prices have really come down on what many people call "PowerPoint Projectors." Choose one that is bright enough for large group viewing, at least 1200 lumens (units indicating brightness).

3. **Powerful speakers.** Laptops are notorious for poor sound quality. If you want your audience to hear audio, like a slide animation sound effect, background music, or video soundtrack, buy speakers that have a good bass end as well as clear treble. I found great factory-refurbished Harman Kardon speakers on eBay, an online auction site, for 40% of their retail value.

4. **A portable screen.** Light colored walls are often adequate surfaces onto which you can project your presentation, but they are hardly portable.

5. **Extension cord and power strip.** Don't leave home without one. You will need power for the projector, speakers, and computer. Although laptop batteries

Setting up for a PowerPoint Presentation

1. Attach the computer (VGA Monitor Out) to the projector (VGA, Monitor, RGB or Computer In). You will need to buy a little video adapter cable for a MacBook.

2. If applicable, plug the speaker into the headphone jack of the computer.

3. Plug the projector, computer, and speakers into the power strip.

4. Turn the computer on last. Then it will sense that it is connected to the projector. If you have a Windows laptop, and the computer screen isn't projected, try pressing function key F5.

5. Change slides by clicking a mouse button, pressing a trackpad button, or pressing down the space bar. You can also use the arrow keys on the keyboard. Many projectors come with remote devices so you do not have to be next to your computer to change slides.

You can also attach a VCR or DVD player to your projector using RCA cables. Then you plug your speakers into the sound out port of the projector. Use the "Source" button on the projector to switch between the projection of video and PowerPoint.

VGA CONNECTOR

RCA PLUGS

are lasting longer, when they run out of juice, they run out of juice. And when you are playing a CD or DVD through your computer for a shared prayer experience, the batteries go faster.

I want...
Online Resources

There are many wonderful sites on the web... and many that are not so good. How does one tell if a Catholic site presents good Catholic theology? What *is* "good Catholic theology"? Without a background in theological education, the average surfer is at the mercy of those who claim their site is "Catholic." A few years ago I heard someone quoting an online Catholic encyclopedia. It wasn't until later that I found out the encyclopedia was from the 1917 edition. It doesn't mean that the resource is worthless, but most would agree that there have been substantial theological developments since then and much of the information presented is dated. Still, I might go to that same site today and find that the webmaster replaced it with a very recent edition, turning a questionable site into a great site.

The Church is big, with many viewpoints from those who are often labeled "liberal" or "conservative." *Good* theology can sometimes be in the eye of the beholder. I have found that if one peruses sites sponsored by official Catholic organizations or institutions, like the Vatican or the United States Conference of Catholic Bishops, one is assured of content that is officially approved. Also, visiting the sites of Catholic universities and religious communities can provide you with trusted ideas and resources.

Other comparatively reliable sources of online content are publishing companies. They have a stake in providing well-developed sites that offer solid content, while updating regularly to keep visitors returning. Some publishers in particular have many free lesson-plan ideas, learning games, printouts of support materials, skits, coloring-book pages, and music. And some religious education series have online resources that correspond to units in their books. Check your curriculum publisher's web site for access to supplemental materials.

EXAMPLES OF RELIGIOUS WEB RESOURCES

1. **Vatican** WWW.VATICAN.VA
   Many official Church documents.

2. **United States Bishops' Conference** WWW.USCCB.ORG
   Searchable New American Bible, movie reviews, and much more.

3. **Catholic News Service** WWW.CATHOLICNEWS.COM
   Searchable collection of news stories, plus "Word to Life" reflections on the Sunday readings.

4. **Paulist** WWW.BUSTEDHALO.COM
   Resources for people in their 20-30s, including a subscribe button to a podcast on faith questions.

5. **The Taizé Community** WWW.TAIZE.FR
Songs with audio tunes, with each part (soprano, bass, etc.) played separately and together.

6. **Irish Jesuits** WWW.SACREDSPACE.IE
Daily lectionary reflections, a favorite of many of my colleagues.

7. **Wing Clips** WWW.WINGCLIPS.COM
Free inspirational clips from Hollywood movies. The free clips are small on the screen, but usable. A paid subscription allows for larger clips for easier viewing.

8. **GodTube** WWW.GODTUBE.COM
This site is for the sharing of Christian videos. Supporters of Maryknoll posted some touching video clips on illegal immigration. Be aware of GodTube's policy on rejecting submissions though, and some of the theology of posted videos (which can, in its own right, lead to some great discussions).

9. **Harcourt Religion Publishers**
WWW.HARCOURTRELIGION.COM
Innovative electronic and online material from this publisher of practical, easy-to-use catechetical programs for Catholic parishes and schools.

10. **Twenty-Third Publications**
WWW.23RDPUBLICATIONS.COM
Terrific resources for faith formation and lifelong catechesis (and my publisher!).

SELECTED SECULAR SITES

1. **Flickr** WWW.FLICKR.COM
   A Yahoo service where you can search for and download pictures for presentations. I found a beautiful picture of a guitar and downloaded it. Rights are reserved under Creative Commons Copyright, a special type of copyright where authors can allow certain uses under specific conditions. I could display the guitar in a liturgical music presentation or brochure for non-commercial uses.

2. **Wikipedia** WWW.WIKIPEDIA.ORG
   A wiki is a collaborative web site that allows people to edit the contents from their web browser. Wikipedia is an online encyclopedia in which the Wikipedia community adds and corrects entries and deletes items that are tastelessly entered as pranks. Many would say that it should only be used as a starting point, since many articles are not verified. Still there are many references, including links to other web sites. It is also a great tool to teach online community and critical thinking.

3. **YouTube** WWW.YOUTUBE.COM
   This site is for the sharing of videos. Food for the Poor (www.foodforthepoor.org) and Covenant House (www.covenanthouse.org) are but a few of many great organizations that are featured in short clips uploaded by their supporters.

4. **del.icio.us social bookmarking** DEL.ICIO.US
   If you like a web site you are visiting, you can "bookmark" it in your browser so you can return later. Del.icio.us is an online bookmarking service that will let you save bookmarks you like online and allow you to give them "tags," or keywords for easy searching. This allows you to use your bookmarks from any computer; share them with your family, friends, and even the wider public, and you can search for bookmarks others have shared.

Using iTunes
(Windows and Macintosh)

While the web has many great resources, it is up to you to go to each of your favorite sites and check to see if there is anything new. And while googling for resources is fun and informative, you need to invest the time to surf. Enter the podcast. A podcast is an audio, video, or even PDF file that is sent to you. You connect to Apple's music store and search their podcast database for a wide range

Finding and subscribing to a podcast

Point your browser to http://www.apple.com/itunes/ download/ and download iTunes. If a podcast isn't in the iTunes directory and you know its web address, you

of topics. If you find a podcast you like, you subscribe to it. From that point on, every time you launch iTunes, it goes through each of your subscriptions, checks for the most recent podcast, downloads it, and lists other available podcasts. Most of the subscriptions I have seen are free. NOTE: to take advantage of podcasts, you do not need an iPod. Podcasting got its name because of the concurrent popularity of Apple's iPod, which works with both Windows and Macintosh. If you download a podcast, you can easily put it on an iPod to carry

can subscribe to it by going to Advanced>Subscribe to Podcast in your menu commands and entering the address.

1. Click on Podcasts

2. Enter Search Criteria

3. Subscribe to the Podcast

with you, thus the name. It is a great tool for anytime, anywhere consumption of great media. I like to watch videos while I am on my exercise machine or listen to audio books or conference keynotes. But, again, you do NOT need an iPod to consume podcasts. Nor do your parishioners need one to listen to, watch, or read your podcasts. In fact, you really don't need iTunes. iTunes is an application that belongs to a class of software called "aggregators." It allows you to "subscribe" to information on the web that is syndicated or made available through a format called Really Simple Syndication (RSS). Go to Google and type in "Feed Aggregator" to find out more about many other free programs. iTunes' specialty is media-rich files, whereas some aggregators are more for text feeds. iTunes is free and very easy to use, and it provides access to a database of wonderful resources (and some that are not so good, thus the need for media literacy formation in catechetical programs). You can also use iTunes to import your music from your CDs and catalogue them on your computer.

Harvesting Text, Graphics, and Multimedia

Lawrence Lessig, in his book, *Free Culture* (www.free-culture.com), presents a fascinating discussion on the protection of intellectual property through copyright. While firmly maintaining the right of an artist and publisher to earn fair compensation for their work, he

Grabbing an image from a web page

1. Windows: Right Click on the image and select "Save Target as" or "Save Picture as" command to save it to your computer. If this command is disabled, you can always use the "Print Screen" button on your keyboard to capture your monitor screen into your clipboard. Then, Edit>Paste it into an application like Paint, and use your graphic tools to crop the image to the part you want.

2. Macintosh: Click on the image and drag it to the desktop. You can also simply drag the photo into an open Word document. If the graphic is protected, you can capture it by holding down the Shift-Command-3 keyboard combination to create a file on your desktop called Picture 1 (or Picture 2 if there is a Picture 1 already, and so on). You can also capture a portion of your screen by pressing Shift-Command-4 and using the resultant crosshair to draw a box around the part you want. In both cases adding the Control key captures the image to your clipboard for quick pasting into applications.

CLICK AND DRAG

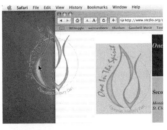

DROP ON THE DESKTOP

argues that an unbalanced legal emphasis on copyright can adversely affect creativity. Examples he cites include Walt Disney's use of the *Fairy Tales of the Brothers Grimm* to produce such landmark works as *Sleeping Beauty* and *Cinderella*. Today using the works of others in this way would raise serious copyright issues. From a moral standpoint, this complex issue is one of justice. An artist is entitled to just compensation. As we look at ways of harvesting online resources we want to keep these things in mind:

1. We are a people of justice, and do not want to steal from others, even if it is "only intellectual property."

2. Copyright laws and protocol allow for "fair use" of resources for certain non-profit educational creations.

3. It behooves us to google "fair use guidelines" and do our own research and err on the side of seeking permission from copyright owners. There is a good resource at American University's Center for Social Media (www.centerforsocialmedia.org/resources/ fair_use).

4. Check into Creative Commons Copyright (creativecommons.org) resources (like many photos on Flickr) for a less-restricted source of multimedia, providing works on a "some rights reserved" basis as opposed to "all rights reserved."

5. Keep an eye on www.feautor.org. This beta site, being developed by a team assembled by Dr. Mary Hess, a Roman Catholic who is teaching at Luther Seminary in St. Paul, Minnesota, promises to provide a place for sharing ecumenical and interfaith religious education resources with Creative Commons Copyrights.

I want...
A Still Camera, Video Camera, or Scanner

Although using available resources from the Internet has many advantages, creating your own still and moving pictures (and audio) can add a stronger dimension to your lesson or discussion. For example, it would be more engaging to talk about baptism with an image of a recent parish baptism than using an anonymous picture from a web site. Digital still cameras are relatively inexpensive, and they can open up a whole new world to catechetical formation. I have a Canon PowerShot A550 7.1MP Digital Camera with 4x Optical Zoom. As of this writing, like many other brands of cameras, it can still be purchased online for under $150. Add another $25 to increase its memory card to one-gigabyte, and you have a very powerful catechetical tool that can store hundreds of photos or nine minutes of full-size video with sound. (Remember, if you can shoot video with sound, you can also record audio and remove the image.) I would

What's in a Name?

Using our **Canon PowerShot A550 7.1MP Digital Camera with 4x Optical Zoom** as an example:

CANON: *Brand Name.* There are many brands from which to choose. I would check reviews at the web sites of major PC or Macintosh magazines like *PCWorld* and *MacWorld.* DCViews (www.dcviews.com) provides a web environment filled with reviews, tutorials, and a discussion forum.

POWERSHOT A550: *Model Name*

7.1MP: *7.1 Mega-pixel.* When I was young, I would use my magnifying glass to look at the photographs in our newspaper, amazed at how a bunch of tiny dots could produce a clear black and white photo. The smaller and the more plentiful the dots were, the clearer the picture. Picture elements (pixels) are like the dots. A 7.1 Mega-pixel camera can take a larger picture with more clarity than a 2 Mega-pixel camera.

DIGITAL CAMERA: Instead of using film, a digital camera stores images as files on a memory card, disk, or some other storage device. The images in many cameras are captured on a charge-coupled device or "CCD." Does that sound familiar? That means that you don't run out of film. It also means that you can do much more with your photos, such as add them to PowerPoint presentations, email them to family, and have them printed as books, calendars, or cards through such services as Apple's iPhoto Print Products or Kodak's EasyShare Gallery. Some services even provide ISBN numbers if you want to sell your photo books.

4X OPTICAL ZOOM: Getting closer or zooming in so that the subject appears closer, four times (4x) closer in this case. With optical zoom, the magnifying quality of your lens keeps the photo focused as you zoom in. Digital zoom is different and less important in considering your purchase. Digital zoom is a camera trick that does exactly the same thing as your photo editing software does when you magnify your photo on your computer. If you zoom in too close, the picture becomes fuzzy or "pixilated."

start with this type of tool to begin exploring ways of integrating multimedia into catechetics.

Digital video (DV) cameras are another great tool and can also be used to take photographs, but the quality of the snapshot is typically not as high. But, if you want to do more with video than a short segment, you will want to invest in one (and a tripod!). Many of the video cameras record on mini-DV tapes, although some now record directly to writable DVD disks and other memory cards or devices. Keep in mind that the tape mechanism will need to be cleaned periodically, and it is fragile. Our old office Canon ZR-10 lost its tape-handling capabilities long ago, but we still plug it directly into our computer and record video directly into Apple's iMovie. Make sure that your camera will work well with your computer. For example, both Microsoft's MovieMaker 2 and iMovie import video easily from cameras that have a type of connection called Firewire. Both of these video-editing programs are free when you buy your computer.

A scanner is used when you have regular photographs or slides (if the scanner is "slide" friendly) to digitize. It can also be used to scan documents, and if it comes with the right software, can turn the document into an editable text file. That would come in handy if you have old policies that need to be updated. You can scan in the policy book and run it through the "optical character recognition" (OCR) program that often comes with the scanner. As mentioned before, there are many printers now that come with a scanner built in. Those can serve as color copiers and some have fax capabilities as well. If you don't have the budget for a scanner, you can always take a snapshot of a photo with your digital camera—with some fairly respectable results.

I want...
Audio

Almost all modern computers come with compact disc (CD) drives and software to play audio CDs. iTunes certainly is one tool that you can use to play music and import songs into your computer. Once you've obtained audio files, you can play them for your small groups straight from your computer's hard drive, or you can embed them in your presentations.

You may also want to record your own audio. If your computer does not have a built-in microphone (many laptops do, as do more and more desktop units), you can buy an inexpensive one if there is a microphone jack. For good quality sound, there are audio input devices that use the same type of port that your keyboard does, called the USB port. To research these tools, google "USB audio input," adding "XLR" if you want to use your regular church microphone.

Audacity is a free sound-processing program you can get at www.download.com. I like that site because it has many free and demo applications for many purposes, and it's easy to remember.

I want...
A Web Presence

As a catechetical leader, I would want a place to post announcements and information for parents, a calendar for students, and exciting classroom photos for the world. I would ask the pastor if he would be interested in writing an online web log (blog) so that parishioners can follow a discussion on connecting with a parish in Kenya, for example. I would ask our pastoral associate to moblog reflections on her ministry from her cell phone. (Moblog is short for Mobile Weblog, or a blog posted from a mobile phone, handheld computer or similar device.) I would want to post registration forms for families to download and announce cancellations in the case of inclement weather. But most of all, I would want a place to exhibit a gallery of students' work, including the images and recordings created with our other tools. Public publishing is a great way to elicit quality work.

> Ask the pastor if he would be interested in writing an online web log (blog) so that parishioners can follow a discussion on connecting with a parish in Kenya, for example.

Steps to establishing a web presence

1. Several companies like Parishes Online and CatholicWeb offer free hosting for parishes (www. parishesonline.com and www.catholicweb.com respectively). You will need to allow a tasteful amount of advertising on the site. You use their online web-building tool, which is limited but easy and quite adequate for most sites. Check also for added free features, like facility scheduling and calendars.

For the more adventurous, and for more flexibility

1. Find space on a web server (a computer that is on 100% of the time with the right software so that people can surf to it anytime). You can check with your parish, parishioners, or diocese to see if there is free space available. If you have your Internet connection through an Internet Service Provider, you often get free space to put your web pages.

2. Buy a Domain name as mentioned above.

3. Learn a program to help you, preferably with a committee of volunteers, to design your site. Microsoft Frontpage for Windows was a common program that was recently discontinued. iWeb for the Macintosh is very easy and free with new Macs, but you are limited to a number of templates. Adobe's DreamWeaver is the professional's choice,

but expensive and has a formidable learning curve. Nvu is a fairly new free program for Windows, Linux, and Macintosh that bears watching (nvudev. com). And Mozilla's Composer is free and easy for simple pages, and is now part of a suite called, of all things, SeaMonkey (www.mozilla.org/projects/seamonkey). Google "composer seamonkey tutorial" for tutorial resources.

Avoiding Catechetical Malpractice

If I were a catechetical leader in a program for "digital natives," I would want to speak their language. Certainly if all my students spoke only Spanish, and I only offered lessons in English, I would be guilty of catechetical malpractice. To use only the methods of the "digital immigrant" is to risk being less than we could be for our young co-journeyers.

6

TOOLS FOR ALL OF US

With a presentation program, online access to harvest resources, and a camera to create multimedia, one has some basic tools to move into the twenty-first century of faith-sharing methods. Why is this so important? To me, the simple answer is engagement. We want to engage others, share our faith, and walk with others as they grow in that faith as disciples of Christ. Multimedia tools serve us at both ends of this process—as tools of instruction in a faith-sharing setting and as tools of proclamation to the whole world.

A decade ago, Lori Dahlhoff, currently the Director of Leadership Formation for Catechesis in Parishes and Schools for the Archdiocese of Saint Paul/Minneapolis, joined seven soon-to-be seventh graders and me for a week of vacation Bible school. Lori and I used a multi-faceted approach to reach out to this vulnerable age group. We had a fairly large classroom that was divided into three separate areas: a prayer environment, a work/

lesson/snack area, and a wall for a few computers for multimedia authoring. Lori employed her rich understanding of Howard Gardner's theory of multiple intelligences, I used my knowledge of Hyperstudio (www.mackiev.com/hyperstudio), the students engaged their creativity, and we all shared our faith.

Gardner's list of intelligences includes:

- Linguistic intelligence ("word smart"):
- Logical-mathematical intelligence ("number/reasoning smart")
- Spatial intelligence ("picture smart")
- Bodily-Kinesthetic intelligence ("body smart")
- Musical intelligence ("music smart")
- Interpersonal intelligence ("people smart")
- Intrapersonal intelligence ("self smart")
- Naturalist intelligence ("nature smart")

—Howard Gardner,
Frames of Mind: The Theory of Multiple Intelligences
(New York: Basic Books, 1997)

Fr. Ronald Nuzzi's book *Gifts of the Spirit: Multiple Intelligences in Religious Education* (NCEA, 2005, 3rd printing; 1999) applies Gardner's theory to religious education. Dr. Thomas Armstrong has a brief explanation of multiple intelligences, including this list, at www.thomasarmstrong.com/multiple_intelligences.htm.

Lori's goal was to create lesson plans that would address as many of these intelligences as possible. My

> I would want tools to proclaim the Good News to all people so they can hear it not only with their ears, but also with their eyes and with their hearts…

goal was to teach a multimedia creation tool that would allow participants to use their differing gifts in ways that would maximize those intelligences. For example, the students reflected on their lives (Intrapersonal Intelligence), and then created an animation (Spatial Intelligence) finishing the statement, "God's Forgiveness is like…" They then shared their creations and affirmed each other's work (Interpersonal Intelligence).

Computers were used only one hour out of each two-and-a-half-hour class, and served only to reinforce the content presented. Even snacks were chosen to supplement the lessons. For example, on the day we talked about finding Moses in the river, Lori whipped up some Rice Krispy treats in the shape of baskets with handles made of pretzels. Multimedia is not limited to technology! The biggest thrill I got was to watch the students sing a song Lori wrote about being a Child of God into a microphone built into the computer. I have never heard kids that age, especially boys, sing with such energy. They would sing, then listen to their recording, and then ask to do it again. "We can do it better," they said. To me, that is engagement.

And their recorded song was evangelization. They became disciples as they used that song to witness to their faith and proclaim what it meant to them to be a Child of God.

The NDC speaks of the inseparable character of evangelization and catechesis.

> Catechesis is so central to the Church's mission of evangelization that, if evangelization were to fail to integrate catechesis, initial faith aroused by the original proclamation of the gospel would not mature, education in the faith through a deeper knowledge of the person and message of Jesus Christ would not transpire, and discipleship in Christ through genuine apostolic witness would not be fostered. (NDC #22)

It would be good to keep in mind three basic stages:

1. The original proclamation of the gospel

2. Education in the faith "aroused" by that proclamation

3. Becoming proclaimers ourselves through witnessing to the gospel

I would want tools to proclaim the Good News to all people so they can hear it not only with their ears, but also with their eyes and with their hearts, using many of the "intelligences" God gave them. I would want tools to help capture their imaginations and then move them to a deeper understanding and life in that faith. Then I would want to give them tools by which they as disciples of Christ can broaden their own "genuine apostolic witness." And very importantly, I would want tools that remind me that I, too, need to be constantly evangelized and catechized, for we are all together on our journey to God.

So as I consider tools for disciples, I choose tools that not only I would use, but that I would want to teach my students, my co-journeyers, to use as we go out to "proclaim the gospel to every creature," even to the ends of the cyber world. And I would start with tools that were multimedia based.

Considerations in using multi-media tools

1. The Word of God is dynamic. So is multimedia. "The medium is the message" (Marshall McLuhan. *Understanding Media: The Extensions of Man.* New York: McGraw Hill, 1964).

2. Computers are to be used to facilitate collaboration and community, not to generate isolation.

3. With multimedia, we can better address multiple intelligences.

4. If we are to create multimedia, we have to employ clear purposeful planning procedures.

5. Integrating technology into our ministry will take time and effort. It's worth it. Remember, it isn't imperative to use technology all of the time, or even most of the time. One project in a year is a good start. If a two-through-seventeen-year-old American child watches an average of twenty-five hours of TV a week, that comes to about 22,100 hours. At roughly thirty-six hours or religious education a year, including preschool programs, students attend 612 hours—if they continue until they are eighteen. Who is telling the "story" that is defining our culture?

6. It is relatively easy to obtain an inexpensive computer (read: donated) and software (read: freeware). A call to the parochial or public school system is a good place to start in researching sources.

The following is my technology wish list for a media'ed disciple, one that can be used in the classroom as well as to reach out to the "ends of the earth."

I want...
Video Production Capabilities
Both iMovie for the Macintosh and MovieMaker for Windows are stable tools for proclaiming the reign of God in ways that captivate our media'ed society.

Using video-editing software can teach our young disciples how to "read" video as well as engage them in their own televangelization. They will learn to think critically as media consumers, separating truth from spin, because they will be struggling to proclaim their own take on truth. They will begin to sense that something isn't necessarily true just because it is on TV or the Internet. And they will learn to speak the language of multimedia to better proclaim the reign of God, even if they start out making some bad videos.

I want...
Audio Production Capabilities

Video files take up a lot of hard-drive space. You can make a "slide show" with audio in a video format that reduces the file size, but it is still very large. If you make DVDs, that may not present a problem, but if you want to broadcast your work on the Internet, size is a huge consideration. This is especially true if much of your audience has a dial-up Internet connection. In such cases, audio-only production is a better option. Other reasons to choose audio over video include:

1. You can broadcast Internet radio programs from your own computer using forty-dollar programs like Nicecast (www.rogueamoeba.com/nicecast) for the Macintosh, or Pirate Radio for Windows (www.pirateradio.com).

Making a video with your youth group

1. Choose your topic, write a "script," and storyboard your production.

   - Storyboarding is laying out, often as a drawing, each scene of the video.
   - Be simple at first.
   - The writing of a script could be done throughout a retreat on a particular theme, or you could build a retreat or unit project around a storyboard.

2. Borrow someone's video camera that is compatible with your computer. Or use a still camera. Ken Burn's did a great job on the PBS series "The Civil War" using still pictures. Some applications like iMovie allow you to pan across a photo, zoom in or zoom out, to give life to a still.

3. Shoot the video or compile the photos. Edit the clips into a seamless movie with titles, transitions, or effects built into your application.

4. Add narration and music as applicable.

5. Watch the video, and if you haven't already done so as a prelude to your project, watch a similar professionally produced video. Compare the two, looking at the techniques used by the director of the professional work. Remember, as we learned to write, we read a lot of books. Re-shoot your video if you like.

6. Distribute it to an appropriate audience.

   - DVD production is becoming easier and more integrated into video-editing software.
   - Save the video as a compressed file, and podcast it, post it on the web, or submit it to YouTube as part of the evangelization work of your youth group. Since it is a file, you can also burn it to a CD or save it on a flash drive and distribute via postal mail.

2. You can record audio books for mp3 players like the iPod.

3. You can produce shows more quickly without worrying about lighting, costumes, and mobile microphones for moving actors, etc.

I want...
A Web Presence

One of the goals of catechesis is to foster "genuine apostolic witness." Through sounds and images we can announce that the reign of God is among us, and through our actions we can make it present at this time and place. The Internet is a huge cyber community that can benefit from such a proclamation. Within that community, we can post videos of our latest Habitat for Humanity project, our favorite celebration at the local night shelter, or our play at the nursing home. We can share poems we wrote about God's face in the smile of a grandparent, or teach viewers how to play their own composition about God's humor on the ukulele. We can broadcast a group's weekly theological reflection on a blockbuster movie, or share why we continue a local custom at our weekend liturgy.

With a web presence as described in the previous chapter, we can post our video and audio stories so that our friends, parishioners, or even the world can come and hear our message. Then, once they sense the power of the Story, they can come back at any time. Of course... they have to come to us. Wouldn't it be great if they set our page as their home page, so that every time they launched their Internet browser, our page came up automatically displaying our latest work? Too bad each browser can only have one home page.

Through sounds and images we can announce that the reign of God is among us, and through our actions we can make it present at this time and place.

Creating a Podcast

As mentioned previously, one can subscribe to podcasts so that every time iTunes is launched, it goes out to a site and checks for new audio, video, or even PDF files. Just as I would want to use iTunes to harvest resources for my catechetical meetings, I would want others to harvest the productions of my parish, and I would hope my students would create media with such innovation and quality that their work would touch many hearts.

Ways of Being Present through Web 2.0

The Internet has offered great resources through web pages, text, pictures, and links to other sites—and maybe a movie or sound clip—for many years now. But

Steps to Audio Podcasting

1. Create a podcast. Use an audio recording program like Garage Band for Macintosh or Audacity (audacity.sourceforge.net) for Windows.

    a. Write a script with your group. Plan it well.

        i. What is the topic?

        ii. Who will provide the voices?

        iii. Who will be the "engineers" and sound editors?

        iv. Will there be music? Is it royalty free?

    b. Record the podcast and add any music prelude or postlude.

    c. Save it as an mp3 file.

2. Upload it to a web server.

3. Add the podcast information to your RSS text file and upload that to your server. PodcastBlaster (www.podcastblaster.com) will walk you through the process and create that file for you.

    a. The RSS file contains information about your organization and about each podcast, including the author, date published, size, and filename.

    b. When launched, iTunes looks at the RSS file to ascertain whether a new podcast has been added since the last time it was launched.

4. Go to Apple's iTunes Store and click on "Podcasts" and then on "Submit a Podcast." Do this just once.

5. When you upload more podcasts, you need to update your RSS file. Remember, if you are going to podcast, you should do so fairly regularly. A subscriber who finds inactivity could get the idea that your organization doesn't care enough to keep adding items, so it may be better not to podcast at all than to start and only have one or two.

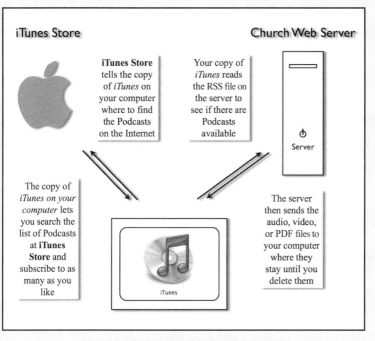

iTunes Store

Church Web Server

iTunes Store tells the copy of *iTunes* on your computer where to find the Podcasts on the Internet

Your copy of *iTunes* reads the RSS file on the server to see if there are Podcasts available

Server

The copy of *iTunes on your computer* lets you search the list of Podcasts at **iTunes Store** and subscribe to as many as you like

The server then sends the audio, video, or PDF files to your computer where they stay until you delete them

iTunes

HOW PODCASTING WORKS WITH iTUNES

now there are new developments that allow for much more sharing and Internet community interaction. This is called Web 2.0, a kind of next-generation version of "Web 1.0." The disciple who goes into this world will find new tools for productivity and information (check out www.google.com/a/ to explore Google's free online applications that include collaboration word processing documents, spreadsheets, and shared calendars), but of special interest to me is the potential for ministry and proclamation. A catechist who has harvested resources for the classroom from selected sites can use these very sites to offer his or her class creations.

1. **Flickr** WWW.FLICKR.COM It would be fun to lead a group of young adults on a photo shoot of the local Habitat for Humanity effort and submit that to Flickr. Or, your group could create a photo meditation on the Stations of the Cross, and upload several photos for each station so others can create a PowerPoint meditation.

2. **Wikipedia** WWW.WIKIPEDIA.ORG You could lead a group of high schoolers in a research project on their local church and enter that into Wikipedia. This could include interviews of retired church leaders. One person submitted the "Ten Commandments of Computer Ethics" (en.wikipedia.org/wiki/Ten_Commandments_of_Computer_Ethics).

3. **YouTube** WWW.YOUTUBE.COM A group of sixth graders could create and upload a video about their

food drive for Catholic Charities. Or they could scan in pictures of God, colored by preschoolers, and set that to narrations by each four-year-old artist. The "cute-factor" is always a draw!

4. **del.icio.us social bookmarking** DEL.ICIO.US Lead your junior-high schoolers on a "webquest" to find great images of Jesus through history and bookmark them for others to find. Of course, you will want to find only quality sites and will therefore need to discuss what constitutes a "quality site."

Challenges and Principles

Web 2.0 also offers other opportunities. Your band of media'ed disciples can join an online social network like Facebook (www.facebook.com) to set up a cyber ministry. Or they can open an account at Blogger.com and post their daily reflections and meditations on theological issues. These ministries open up a whole arena of questions and concerns, and they underscore the need for us to walk with one another in a loving community.

Recalling John Staudenmaier's reflection on Jesus saying, "I love them. Will you go out to them with me?" I ask myself, "Go where?"

> ...87% of those between the ages of 12 and 17 are online. (Pew Internet & American Life Project, www.pewinternet.org/PPF/r/162/report_display.asp)

More than half (fifty-five percent) of all online American youths ages twelve to seventeen use online social networking sites, according to a new national survey of teenagers conducted by the Pew Internet & American Life Project. (Pew Internet & American Life Project, www.pewinternet.org/PPF/r/198/report_display.asp)

Also growing is the number of other age groups that are online. Is our Church there? How do we reach out to the growing cyber community in safe, effective, and theologically sound ways? I don't know. I am a novice missionary in the online world. It is so new.

Still, I would like to offer thoughts about some principles and the challenges they present.

1. **If it isn't about relationship building, it isn't about ministry.** I still hear educators express concern about solitary students at computers with earphones, isolated from classmates. While we need to be aware that some isolation can occur, technology really has the power to foster collaboration and community. Where is the Church in this dynamic?

2. **Internet Safety is paramount.** With so many stories of online cyber bullying, exploitation, and sexual harassment, we need to teach safety skills to our young, and exercise care as adult disciples. (Nebraska's Education Service Unit 13 has a list of online safety sites at dl.esu13.org/internetsafety.

htm.) Jesus sent disciples out in pairs; that should give us some direction. We need to know, work with, and possibly help develop parish and diocesan "Safe Environment" policies so that ministry can take place safely, even online.

> We need to teach safety skills to our young, and exercise care as adult disciples.

3. **If everyone can publish, could it be the same as no one publishing?** There are millions of blogs and web sites. Who will visit them unless a trusted person recommends them? I rarely surf through the videos on YouTube, but I always check out video links that my daughters email me, trusting that I will enjoy them.

   After a diocesan presentation I gave on podcasting, the leader of the group reminded everyone: "This doesn't mean we can quit going out to parishes." I would agree. In fact, we have to intensify our personal relationships with parishes so that they will want to subscribe to our podcasts, blogs, and web sites, and recommend them to others.

4. **Address the multiple intelligences of your audience.** With multimedia, we can engage the affective level of the listener, if we know how. We

need to know how. Our ministry is to the whole person.

5. **Copyright Issues.** How can we protect the livelihood of artists and at the same time foster the ability of others to build on their creativity without the threat of lawsuits?

6. **Ecological and environmental issues.** I have several computers in my office that work perfectly well; except that they are so old they don't run the software needed for connection to other people. I can't use them, and I cannot find anyone who will. They will become waste, even if much of each machine is recycled. There is a movement launched by Greenpeace International to pressure computer companies to make their computers as "green" as possible. You can send an email to several computer manufacturing CEOs by filling out a form at http://www.greenpeace.org/international/news/greening-of-apple-310507/greencomputerchallenge.

7. **Technology is a moving target.** Since this writing, web sites cited in this book have changed. Microsoft's Vista has been improved. Apple's Leopard has been released. The moment I learn a program well enough to train others, there is a new version available. Once I have finished a group email list, someone changes his or her address. How does one keep up?

8. **Stress.** See Numbers 6 and 7.

9. **When NOT to use technology.** Sometimes the decision to use technology is an art, a developing art, and not a set of hard-and-fast rules. I heard a presenter once say that there is no place in a sanctuary for a projection screen. Ever. Yet my own parish built a screen for backlit projection that is the same classic beige color as the rest of the sanctuary wall, and it blends into the wall when there are no hymn lyrics or pictures projected. During the Easter Vigil's proclamation of the creation story, there were slides of nature corresponding to the seven days. Is this appropriate? Can it be a gaudy display of techie showiness today and a very real aid to prayer tomorrow?

What about the use of email instead of a phone call? Should one send a Catholic e-card (www.catholicgreetings.org) or buy and mail an anniversary card?

I don't know the answers here. I have a sense of what works and what doesn't for me, but, once

> Sometimes the decision to use technology is an art, a developing art, and not a set of hard-and-fast rules.

again, those decisions are for communities to grapple with.

So when Jesus says, "I love *them*. Will you go out to *them* with me?" we can say "yes." We can say "yes" even if *they* have *their* noses at a computer screen. We can say "yes" even if *they* have a cell phone to their ear while driving. We can say "yes" even if *they* are the Nick Burnses of the technological elite. We can say "yes" because we have one another, we have tools to use, we have a community for support, and because we have the reign of God to make present and to proclaim, even to the ends of the earth. Even to the ends of the cyber world!

AIFF: Ubiquitous sound file format. If you do audio, you will often work with this common format.

ASCII Text: Text only. Word files contain information to format text (columns, italics, indents, etc.) ASCII Text is just text. Email is often in this format.

AUP: Acceptable Use Policy. If your students will be using computers, especially for web searches, create an AUP for them to read and sign with their parents. This should include parental permission to use their works and images as outlined in the policy. Check your local schools for samples.

Backup: If your hard drive crashes right now, will you lose your data? Backup! Backup! Backup!

Bandwidth: Amount of data your Internet Connection can pass. If you want to enjoy or produce multimedia over the web, you will want a fast connection, plenty of Bandwidth.

Bcc: Blind Carbon Copy. Email address field to send a copy to someone without other recipients seeing who it is.

Beta: Application or web site that is public for testing, but not quite finished.

Blog: Short for Web Log. Online journal or diary, often with an opportunity for readers to send in their reactions.

Blogosphere: The total collection of blogs. Some researchers are beginning to see blogs as one way of taking the pulse of world opinion.

Blu-ray: Blu-ray is an optical disc format like a DVD, but with about five times the capacity.

BMP: Bitmap. Graphic file made of dots arranged to make a picture.

Bookmark: When you find a web page you like, you can bookmark it in your browser to go back to it. Teachers will often bookmark pages for their students so lesson time isn't spent searching.

Bps: Bits per Second. A measurement of data transfer speed. Faster is better. Dial up connections offer up to 56,000 bps, but that is too slow for viewing online video comfortably.

Broadband: Think of it as Internet access that is fast enough for most online activity.

Browser: The program you use to surf (visit and browse) the Internet.

Buffering: Quickly receiving and storing audio or video data so it plays more smoothly.

Burn: Writing files or multimedia to a Compact Disk (CD) or Digital Video Disks (DVD).

Cable Modem: The device you get from the cable company for Internet connection.

CC: Carbon Copy. Email address field for sending a copy to someone. Other recipients can see who it is.

CD, CD-R, CD+R, CD-RW: Compact Disc. CD-Rs and CD+Rs can be written to once. Be aware that some drives require -R or +R. Check your manual. CD-RWs can be written to several times, but aren't as reliable. Some music CD players prefer CD-R to CD-RW.

Content Filter: A means of restricting what can be seen in your browser. While not 100% effective, it keeps a lot of inappropriate sites from being accessible.

Creative Commons Copyright: A form of copyright that promotes sharing and creativity over a strict financial bottom line.

Cross-platform: Compatible with Windows, Macintosh, Unix, or other Computer Systems. Since "it is all about communicating," it is good to purchase software that is cross-platform when possible.

CRT: Cathode Ray Tube. A computer monitor that is similar to old TVs.

Cyber: Prefix describing what or who is part of the computer or information age.

Database: Think rolodex with pizzazz!

Desktop: When you first turn on your computer, you are looking at your desktop.

Domain Name: Internet name, e.g. www.domain.org

Download: Receive files from files on a server or the Internet, e.g., you download video data to watch clips.

Driver: Software to make something work. A common fix to printer problems is to download and install the latest "driver" from the company's web site.

DSL: Digital Subscriber Line. A type of fast Internet connection.

DV: Digital Video. DV cameras that use mini-DV tapes are a good choice for video production.

DVD: Digital Video or Versatile Disk. DVD-Rs and DVD+Rs can be written to once. Be aware that some drives require -R or +R, so check your manual. DVD-RWs can be written to several times, but aren't quite as reliable.

EPS: Encapsulted Postscript. A type of graphic file appropriate for Postscript printers. Liturgists often create these files with Finale, a program that produces music and lyrics for worship aids.

Ethernet: Type of network that allows computers to talk to each other and the Internet.

External Hard Drive: Comparatively inexpensive drive you can temporarily hook up to your computer to backup your files. (Then you can take the drive to someplace safe off site.)

FAQ: Frequently Asked Questions.

Field: When thinking "rolodex," think one data item like a first name of someone.

File: Any discreet digital document, video, audio or graphic, etc. that is on your drive.

File Extension: The three letters at the end of a filename that indicates what kind of document is it, e.g., if a filename ends in .doc, you know it is Microsoft Word compatible.

Firefox: A cross-platform web browser preferred by many users.

Firewall: Software or hardware that protects your

online computers from being reached by cyber-bad guys.

Firewire: The type of connection used to transfer data, especially video data, from cameras, external drives, etc.

Flash: Adobe's web technology for animation, both interactive and view-only and video. Some publishers have Flash games to reinforce their catechetical units.

Freeware: Software that is free to use. Sometimes it is worth what you pay, but often there are great tools given generously by the online community.

FTP: File Transfer Protocol. A way of sending files through the web. Web design programs often have this built in to transfer pages you create to the computer that hosts your web site.

GIF: Graphic file type that is small, can be animated, and allows for transparent backgrounds. Great for web site logos and other graphics that require 256 colors or less.

Gigabyte: GB. A bit is a 0 or 1 in computer language. A byte is 8 bits. A GB is a billion bytes, roughly 255 mp3 songs or lots and lots and lots of Word documents!

Gigahertz: One billion clock ticks per second. The higher the number of clock ticks, the faster computer commands are executed. Faster is better, especially in multimedia production.

Gmail: Google's free mail service.

Google: A popular search engine. You put in criteria for a search, and it gives you web sites that have information about your keywords. Google is developing many more online tools than just the search engine. Keep an eye on them.

Hard Disk or Drive: The disk that stores your documents when the computer is turned off.

Home Page: First page people see when they launch their browser. It is also a term for a site's main web page.

Host: Machine that stores your web site or other web information.

Hotmail: Microsoft's free email service that is integrated with its Instant Messenging service.

HTTP: Hyper Text Transfer Protocol. The method by which data is transferred to be translated by your browser into readable, and often pleasing, web pages.

Hyperstudio: Wonderful program for students to create multimedia.

IM: Instant Messaging. By using certain programs like Apple's iChat and Windows Messenger, one can communicate instantly with others who are concurrently online.

IMAP: Internet Message Access Protocol. A form of email that leaves messages on the server to be accessed again from another computer.

iMovie: Apple's free video editing software.

Inkjet Printer: Printer that "bubbles" ink on pages. Sharp, colorful, but expensive to print per page.

Internet Explorer: A free "Windows only" browser for surfing the web.

IP Address or Number: Internet Protocol. Think "telephone number" assigned to a computer to communicate in a network or on the Internet.

iPod: Apple's MP3 player that can also play videos, slide shows, and games. It syncs easily to podcasts and other audio and video files using iTunes. You can buy add-ons, like a microphone to record directly onto it, or a cable to play videos to a TV or LCD projector.

ISP: Internet Service Provider. The company that connects you to the Internet.

iTunes: Free cross-platform application to play your CDs, subscribe to podcasts, view videos, and categorize all of these files.

JPG or JPEG: Joint Photographic Experts Group. Good graphic format for online photos because it can support 16 million colors.

Keyboard Shortcut: You can find keyboard shortcuts in your drop-down menus to streamline your work so you aren't constantly reaching for your mouse.

LAN: Local Area Network. Your office network is a LAN.

LCD Projector: Liquid Crystal Display Projector. This is a catchall term for what people often call

"PowerPoint Projectors." DLP (Digital Light Processing) and LCoS (Liquid Crystal on Silicon) are newer technologies providing the same service of projecting images from computer screens, VCRs, and DVD players.

Listserv: An email list service where subscribers can receive and often send topical email to large groups of people.

Mac OS X: Apple's Operating System that runs Macintosh computers. The X is the Roman numeral ten.

Malware: Malicious software that damages or disables computers or computer systems, e.g., viruses.

Megapixel: One million picture elements, the "dots" that make up a picture. The higher the number, the more refined the picture.

Modem: Short for "modulator-demodulator." Device that allows your computer or network to talk to the Internet.

MovieMaker: Microsoft's free video editing software.

MP3: Audio format. Good quality in small file sizes.

MPG or MPEG: Moving Picture Experts Group. One file format for video.

Multiple Intelligences: Howard Gardner's theory that everyone has many intelligences. Some can be more developed than others.

Network: The connection of computers so they can talk to each other and the Internet, usually using Ethernet cables or wireless.

OCR: Optical Character Recognition. The process by which software analyzes a scanned document and turns words into editable text.

OS: Operating System. Software that lets programs talk to the computer itself at the most basic level, e.g., when you save a Word document, the operating system directs the computer to save it to a disk.

PDF: Portable Document Format. Adobe's technology that displays and prints a document as it was meant to look, regardless of platform.

Peripheral: Printer, scanner, or some other device connected to your computer system.

Plain text: Text only. Word files contain information to format text (columns, italics, indents, etc.) so it is not plain text. Email is often in this format.

Platform: Type of computer and operating system used. Windows on a PC and Mac OS X on a Macintosh are two common platforms.

PNG: Portable Network Graphics. Graphic format that allows for transparency and control over opacity on the web, but is not supported by all browsers.

Podcast: A regular audio or video broadcast that you can subscribe to through iTunes for Windows or Macintosh.

POP Account: Post Office Protocol. An account that downloads email to your computer when you check it. You can save your email for documentation, but you cannot go to another computer and check the same messages again, since they now reside on the first computer.

PostScript: A cross-platform language that many printers use to create smooth documents.

PowerPoint Projector: See LCD projector.

RAM: Random Access Memory. The electronic memory a computer uses to think.

RCA plugs: Round plugs to connect DVD players and VCRs to a projector.

Record: When thinking "rolodex," think of one card with all the information about a single household.

RGB: Red, Green, Blue. RGB refers to a system for representing colors. You may see it as a label on a port to connect a computer to a monitor or projector.

Robots: Programs that search the web for information. They can be good, keeping search engines up to date, or bad, harvesting posted email addresses for spammers.

Router: A device that "routes" data to specific computers. In the case of an office network, the router is connected to the Internet via a cable modem to direct a web page to the computer that asked for it.

RSS: Really Simple Syndication. Formats that allow

for text, audio, and video files to be "fed" to users when they subscribe to them. Podcasts are a type of "rss feed."

RTF: Rich Text Format. A common text file that also includes instructions for simple formatting like text styles and paragraph format. Almost all word processing programs can open and "save as" these files.

Safari: Apple's cross-platform web browser.

Scanner: A device, now often built into an inkjet printer, which scans a document for faxing, copying, digitizing, or turning the text into an editable document.

Server: A computer whose only purpose is to "serve up" files. A typical web server stores and sends out web pages 24/7.

Shareware: Software that is free to try, but the programmer often asks for a modest fee if you decide to keep it.

SIT: Compression method for a Macintosh to make files smaller for emailing or archiving.

Social bookmarking: Site where people can share their favorite web bookmarks in searchable categories.

Social networking: Site where people can post personal information as well as musings, photos, blogs, videos, etc., and allow others to meet them. There are often varying levels of security, and people can form online communities of common interests.

Spam: Unsolicited junk email.

Spreadsheet: Think financial ledger with lots of cells for each number or formula.

Spyware: Program that sneaks onto your computer and sends personal information to a bad guy through the Internet.

System Requirements: When buying software make sure it will run on your computer by checking these in the software information.

TCP/IP: Transfer Control Protocol/Internet Protocol. Protocols that give your computer an address and capability to be on a network or the Internet.

TIFF: Tagged Image File Format. Good graphic format for printing, but too large to be supported by web browsers.

Trojan Horse: Malware that looks safe but does bad things in the background.

Upload: Send files to a server, transfer data to another computer system; e.g., you can upload video data for others to watch.

URL: Uniform Resource Locator. Internet address.

USB: Universal Serial Bus. Allows for the connection of devices like a mouse, keyboard, camera, printer, scanner, flash drive, etc., to your computer through the USB port.

VGA: Virtual Graphics Array. A type of graphics adapter. You may see it as a label on a port to connect a computer to a monitor or projector.

Virus: Malware than can replicate itself to attack other computers through email, shared disks, etc.

VOIP: Voice Over Internet Protocol. Technology that allows you to use the Internet like a telephone.

Glossary

VPN: Virtual Private Network. Technology that allows you to join your private office network from home.

WAN: Wide Area Network. Network of computers separated by long distances. The web is an example.

Web 2.0: A term that refers to advanced and interactive web technologies, like collaborative editing tools, social networking, online photo editing software, interactive games, etc.

Web Host: A machine or company that serves your web pages to the world.

Webmail: Email through a web page, e.g., you can check your Gmail account from any machine connected to the Internet, using any good browser.

Wi-Fi: Wireless Fidelity. Wireless networking technology. If you have a wireless card in your laptop, you can go to a Wi-Fi cafe and browse the Internet without using a cable to hook up to their network.

Wiki: Web space that is editable. Great for collaborative work, where a committee can author and edit a document through the Internet.

Windows: Microsoft's Operating System that runs IBM compatible computers (often called PCs for "personal computers").

Wireless: Think office networking without the cables.

Word Processor: Software for typing letters and other documents. Microsoft Word is a common example.

WYSIWYG: What You See (on the screen) Is What You Get (in the finished product).

XLR Connector: Three prong connector used by most church microphones.

Yahoo!: A popular search engine like Google, and they, too, are developing many more online tools. Check them out!

ZIP: Compression method to make files smaller for emailing or archiving.

*The following is a list of the web sites
mentioned in this book.
See also pages 59-60 for a list of religious web sources.*

Adobe www.adobe.com

Apple www.apple.com

Atomic Learning www.atomiclearning.com

Audacity www.download.com

Catholic E-cards www.catholicgreetings.org

Center for Social Media at American University
www.centerforsocialmedia.org

Consistent Computer Bargains, Inc.
www.1ComputerBargains.com

Creative Commons Copyright
creativecommons.org

DCViews www.dcviews.com

del.icio.us social bookmarking del.icio.us

Dr. Thomas Armstrong
www.thomasarmstrong.com